Bachpan
Childhood
The Gift of God

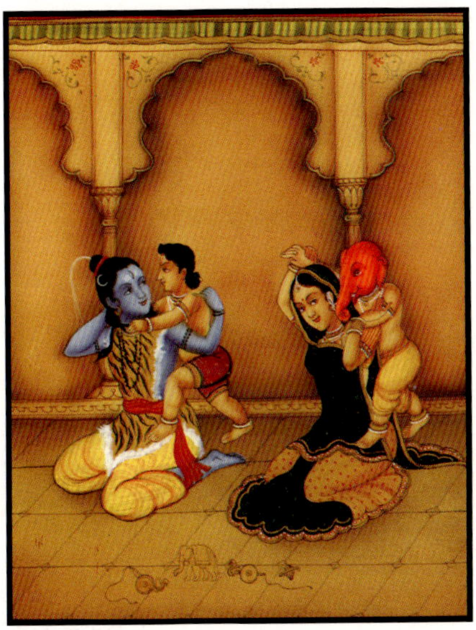

R.N. Kogata • Lalita Kogata

D.K. Printworld (P) Ltd.
New Delhi

Cataloging in Publication Data — DK
[Courtesy: D.K. Agencies (P) Ltd. <docinfo@dkagencies.com>]

Kogaṭā, Rāma, 1964-
Bachpan = Childhood : the gift of god / R.N. Kogata, Lalita Kogata.
p. cm.
English and Hindi; parallel text.
ISBN 13: 9788124605967
ISBN 10: 8124605963

1. Children — Prayers and devotions. 2. Children in art. 3. Gaṇeśa (Hindu deity) — Art. 4. Siva (Hindu deity) — Art. 5. Parvati (Hindu deity) — Art. 6. Hindu art. I. Kogaṭā, Lalitā, 1965-, joint author. II. Title. III. Title: Childhood : the gift of god.

DDC 704.9425 22

First Published in India, 2011
ISBN 13: 978-81-246-0596-7
ISBN 10: 81-246-0596-3

A Creation of:
Mr. R.N. Kogata
Mrs. Lalita Kogata
608, Hiran Magari, Sector-11, Udaipur - India
Phone : +91-94141-58870, +91-294-2583870
devkush@rediffmail.com

Published and printed by:
D.K. Printworld (P) Ltd.
'Vedaśrī', F-395, Sudarshan Park
Ramesh Nagar Metro Stn., New Delhi - 110 015 - 11
Phs.: 011-2545 3975, 2546 6019
Fax: 011-2546 5926
Email: indology@dkprintworld.com
Web: www.dkprintworld.com

बचपन
Bachpan
Childhood
The Gift of God

आलक्षदन्तमुकुलान्यनिमित्तहासैरव्यक्तवर्णरमणीयवचः प्रवृत्तीन् ।
अङ्काश्रयप्रणयिनस्तनयान् वहन्तो, धन्यास्तदङ्गरजसा मलिनीभवन्ति ॥

— अभिज्ञानशाकुन्तलम् - ७.१७

अकारण हँसने से जिनकी दन्तकलियाँ कुछ-कुछ दिखलाई पड़ती हैं और अस्पष्ट वर्णोच्चारण (तोतली बोली) के कारण जिनका बोलना मनोरम लगता है, तथा जो गोद में रहने के लिए लालायित रहते हैं, ऐसी संतति को गोद में धारण करने वाले भाग्यवान् लोग ही उनके शरीर की धूलि से सुशोभित होते हैं ।

Blessed indeed are those parents who get soiled with the dust of the infantile limbs of their little children while carrying them, and the children are fondly seeking refuge in their parents' laps, having buds of teeth partially visible by their innocent, causeless laugh and whose speech sounds charming while they try to articulate words in their indistinct voice.

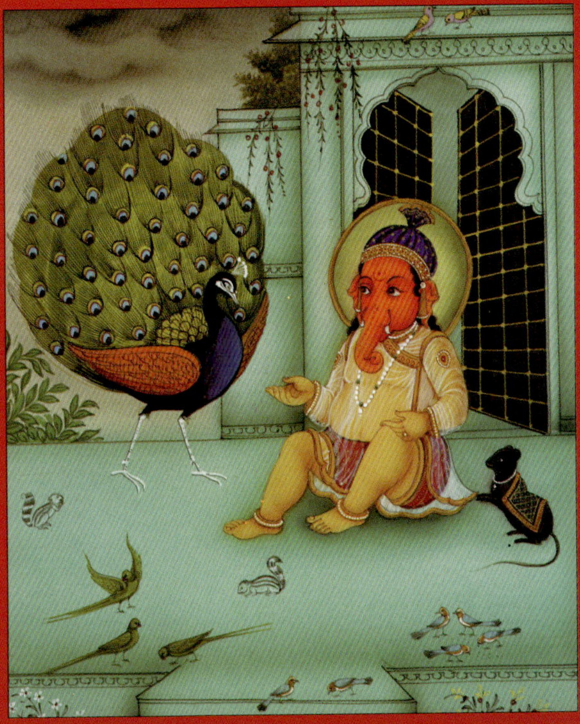

॥ ॐ गं गणपतये नमः ॥

Preface

As a plant is proud to bear its golden wheat, there is no better wealth for parents than children's feats? Children are like buds of flowers. Nourish them with good thoughts, feed them on quality education, and they would turn into a valley of flowers.

What a joy it is to see children walk and learn to move, to utter sounds with sense; what joy it is to hear their mental stores and to see them worldly wise, avoid nonsense; what joy to see the child, father of man and what joy to see them outdo their parents; what joy when things we cannot do, they can and what joy to see their God-given talents.

The greatest joy on earth is our children. The children are the apple of parents' eyes; to see them well is parents' only aim; so, parents slog all life to make them wise; their minds are filled with joy when they get fame.

Little children are love, little children are gift, little children are blessings, little children teach us much, and little children are God in itself. Their smile brings spring and their tears the monsoon and they are the hope and future, if they are allowed to bloom.

Children are God's way of extending time; there's no greater treasure that you can find. He picked a unique way to say. Without children, where would the world be? Who would be there? Who would be there to see? Nature in its beauty has the lakes, the trees, the fields, the flowers, the animals, and even the air we feel. God made children so that we would know how beautiful life can be if we continue to grow.

A child has serene heart, a calm face, an immutable thought, love and friendship for all, he is innocent and honest and shines the whole family with flash and illumination, the child represents the Almighty himself. As such, you cannot enter heaven unless you become like little children. So let's bless our little children as they grow from day-to-day.

Remember, the older you grow, the more earnestly you feel that the few joys of childhood are the best that life has to give and you will always recall and recollect that childhood is the best time in anyone's life.

Inspired by these lovely and heart-touching characteristics about child and childhood, this book is a small try by us to express our thoughts and love for the childhood with the expectation of blessing from all of you.

Our journey would miss out an important part, if we do not express our whole-hearted love, affection and gratitude for our friends, specially Shri Raj Kumar Goel from Mumbai and our family members, who have been motivating us in our creativity and work.

We prostrate towards our parents, Smt. Kanchan Devi Kogata and Shri Bhairav Lal Kogata, and Smt. Kamla Devi Nuwal and Late Prof. K.M. Nuwal, for their beloved blessings for reaching at this stage.

With the expectation of blessings and constructive feedback from all of you.

R.N. Kogata
Lalita Kogata

Importance of Childhood

"Blessed be childhood, which brings down something of heaven into the midst of our rough earthliness."

— Henri Frederic Amiel

"Backward, turn backward, O Time, in your flight, make me a child again, just for tonight!"

— Elizabeth Akers Allen

According to Hindu thought, our patriarchal lineage comes to a stop if there is no son born in the family. To be blessed with a child, what all people do! — go round *ashvattha* and neem trees, do pilgrimages, conduct *sarpa-dosha-parihaara*s, do *pinda-daana* at Rameswaram to please the forefathers, organise *putrakaameshti yajna* like King Dasharatha, and so on.

In our epics and Puraanas there are many instances where a *bhakta* prays to Lord Vishnu (mostly) that the Lord should be born as a child to him in his next birth. There is an interesting episode in the Puraanas. We all know that Lord Rama has special affection towards Kaikeyi. When Rama was ruling Ayodhya, he wanted to know from his mother if there was still any desire to be fulfilled by him. He went to Kaikeyi first and asked, "Mother, do you have any desire to be fulfilled by me?" Kaikeyi said, "Yes, Rama, you should spend your childhood years with me in my next birth." Rama agreed. Then he went to his mother Kausalya and asked the same question. Kausalya said, "You should be born in my womb in my next birth." Rama again agreed. Being divine promises, Rama in his next *avataara* as Krishna was born to Devaki (Kausalya in her next birth), but spent his childhood years from day one in Yasoda's (Kaikeyi's next birth) house to her utter delight.

Once Yasoda was giving bath to little Krishna by putting him stomach-down on her legs and massaging his back — a sight you can see in our villages even now. At that time all the *deva*s assembled in the sky and exclaimed, "When we are offering prayers, flowers, etc. and doing penance to catch a glimpse of the Lord's feet, what *tapas* did Yasoda do by which the Lord is holding her legs tight? Really a blessed soul she is."

Another episode from the Puraanas shows that even kicks from a child's feet are taken as blessings of God. In an effort to prove the greatness of Lord Vishnu, sage Bhrigu, who was slighted by both Brahma and Shiva, went to Vaikuntha. Vishnu was lying on his serpent bed as usual. Bhrigu went straight to Vishnu and gave him a kick on his chest. Vishnu immediately held Bhrigu's foot, asked if it didn't hurt him, and started massaging it. Because of his kindness and concern for one who had kicked him, Vishnu was adjudged the most benevolent of the three gods. Goddess Lakshmi, who always resides in the chest of Vishnu, got offended with Bhrigu's action. To calm and please her, Bhrigu fell at her feet, sought pardon, and prayed that, to avenge the kick, she should be born as a daughter to him and give him as many kicks as she wants with her tiny baby feet. This sight also you must have witnessed — grandfather or father sitting in an easy chair holding the baby aloft and the tiny one jumping and kicking the man's chest all the time giggling — pleasure incomparable to anything else in the world.

When a baby is born in our family, we all wonder, "How delicate the skin, how sweet is the breath of the child!" (Europides in *Medea.*) The whole family's attention is centred around the child after it completes one year and takes baby steps in an effort to walk. When it walks or runs or cries or blabbers, all the members of the family rejoice over its antics and pranks. When it is two to three years old, we enjoy dressing it in the finest of clothes and take pride in holding its hand and walking. In our villages children up to the age of five are considered incarnations of gods themselves and they are not allowed to prostrate before others! such is the importance we give to little children!! When we see little boys and girls finely dressed shouting, screaming, running, fighting, becoming friends the next moment — all innocent beings like just-bloomed flowers — how we wish that they be "frozen for all time" in their pristine beauty and innocence! (ludicrous thought, we all know).

After childhood, adolescence, teenage and adulthood, retired old men and women always wish they became children again and enjoyed their childhood days in their small villages and towns. Old people often remember and talk about their childhood days rather than their teenage and adulthood. It shows how important a part childhood plays in a human life — why, in animal life as well; you must have enjoyed the scenes in which little kittens, puppies, kids, calves, etc. play and frolic among themselves — they are also gifts of God. Rabindranath Tagore said, "Life's aspirations come in the guise of children."

O Time, make us children again just for a few days!

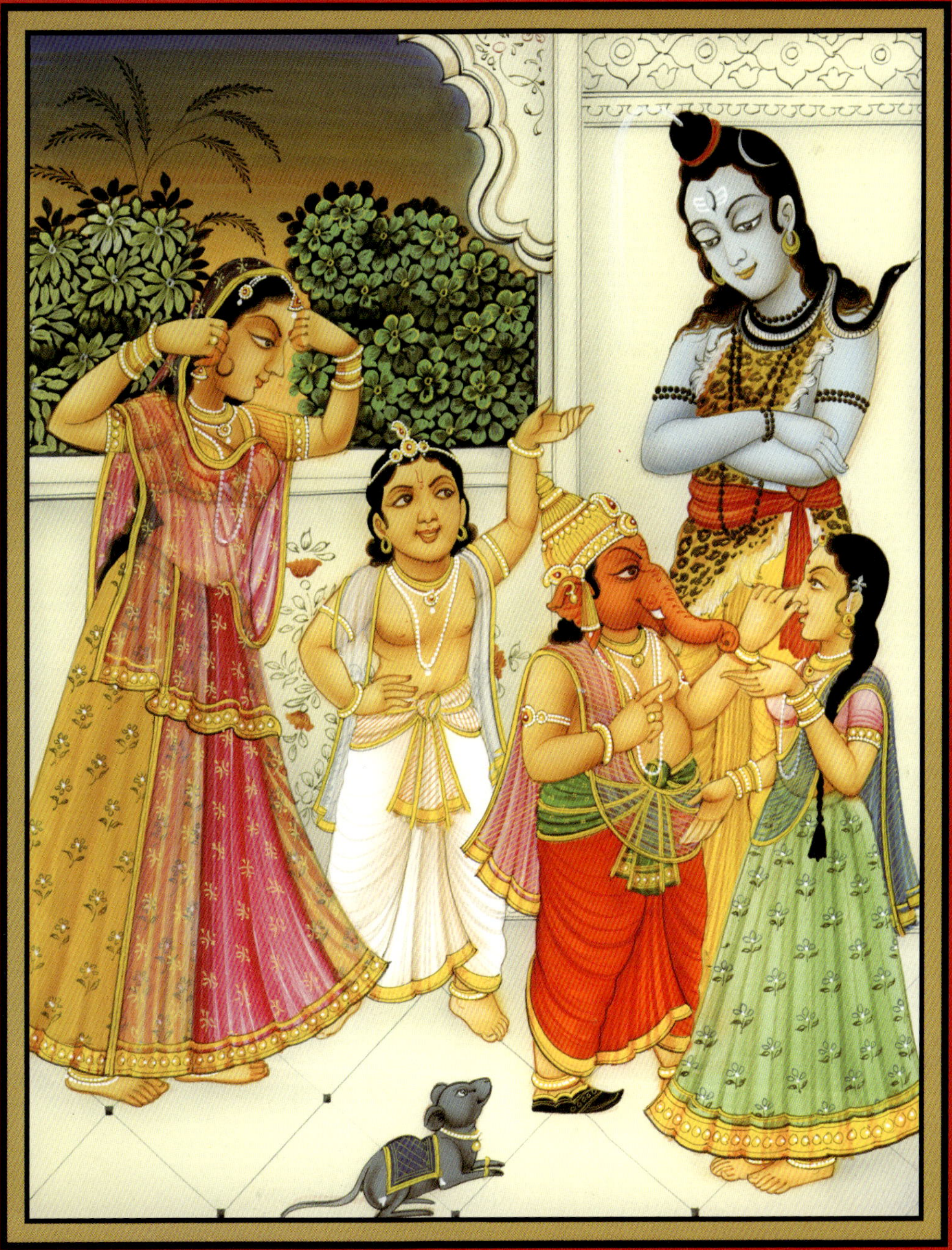

बचपन माँ का हृदय है, पिता की आशा है।
बचपन बहन का सपना है, भाई का ठहाका है।।

बचपन
Bachpan
Childhood

Childhood is the heart of mother and expectations of father.
Childhood is the dream of sister and cachinnation of brother.

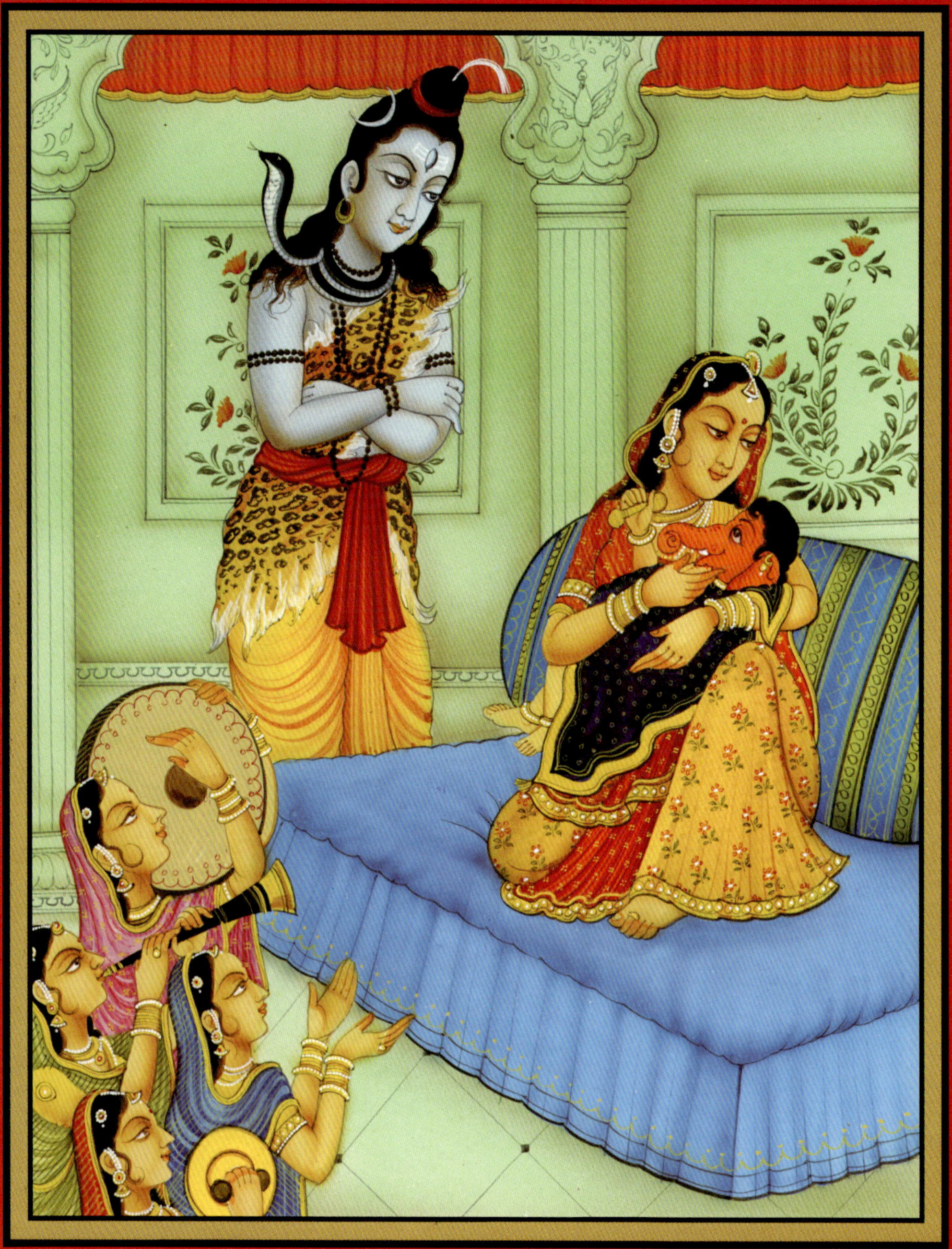

बचपन का आना घर में खुशियों की आहट है।
बचपन से हर परिवार में हंसी और मुस्कुराहट है।।

बचपन
Bachpan
Childhood

Childhood's arrival is sound of footstep of cheerfulness.
Childhood provides laughs and smiles to the whole family.

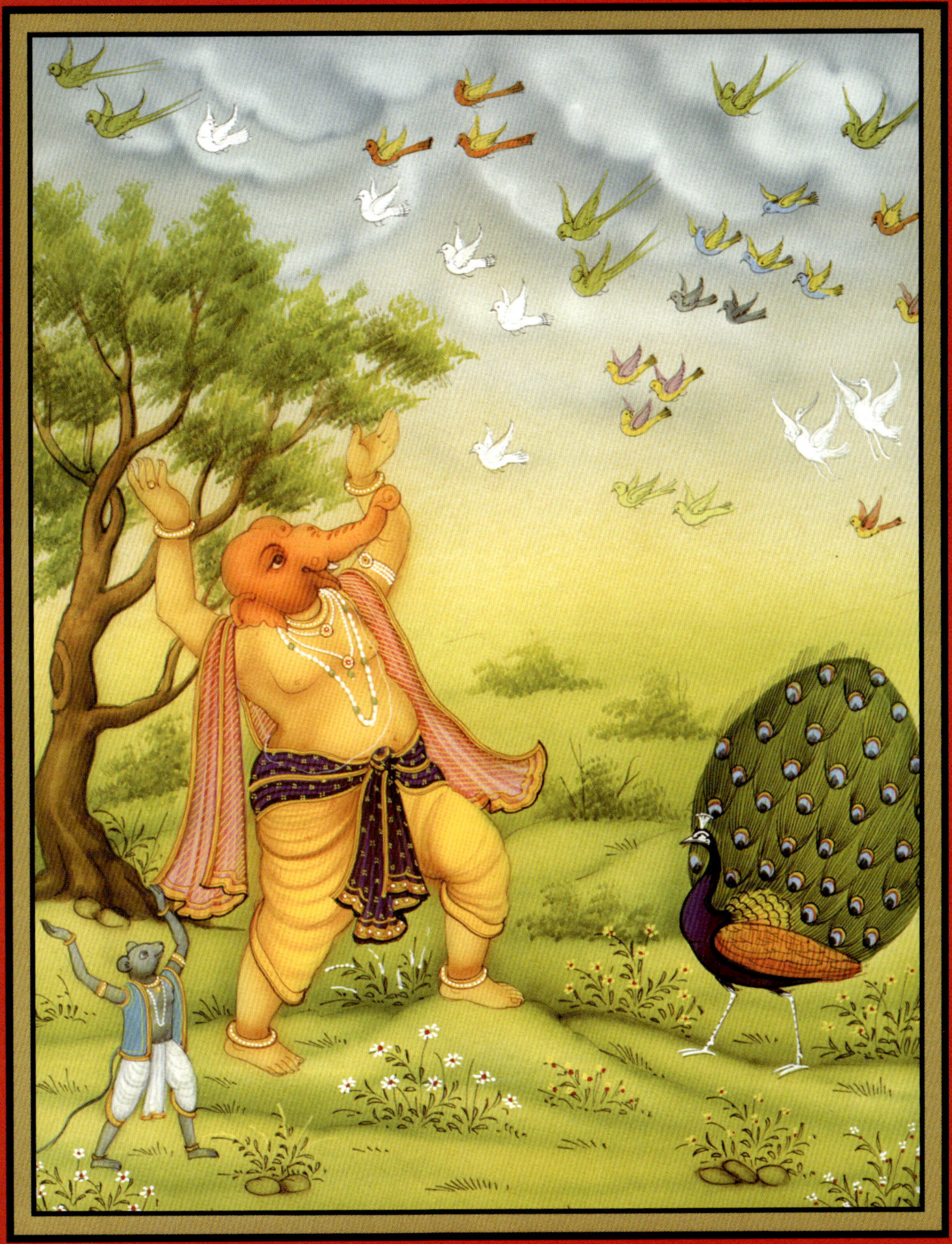

बचपन खुले आसमान का छोटा सा परिन्दा है।
बचपन की किलकारियों से ही खुशियाँ ज़िन्दा हैं।।

Childhood is a small bird of the huge blue sky.
Childhood's sound of joy keeps the happiness alive.

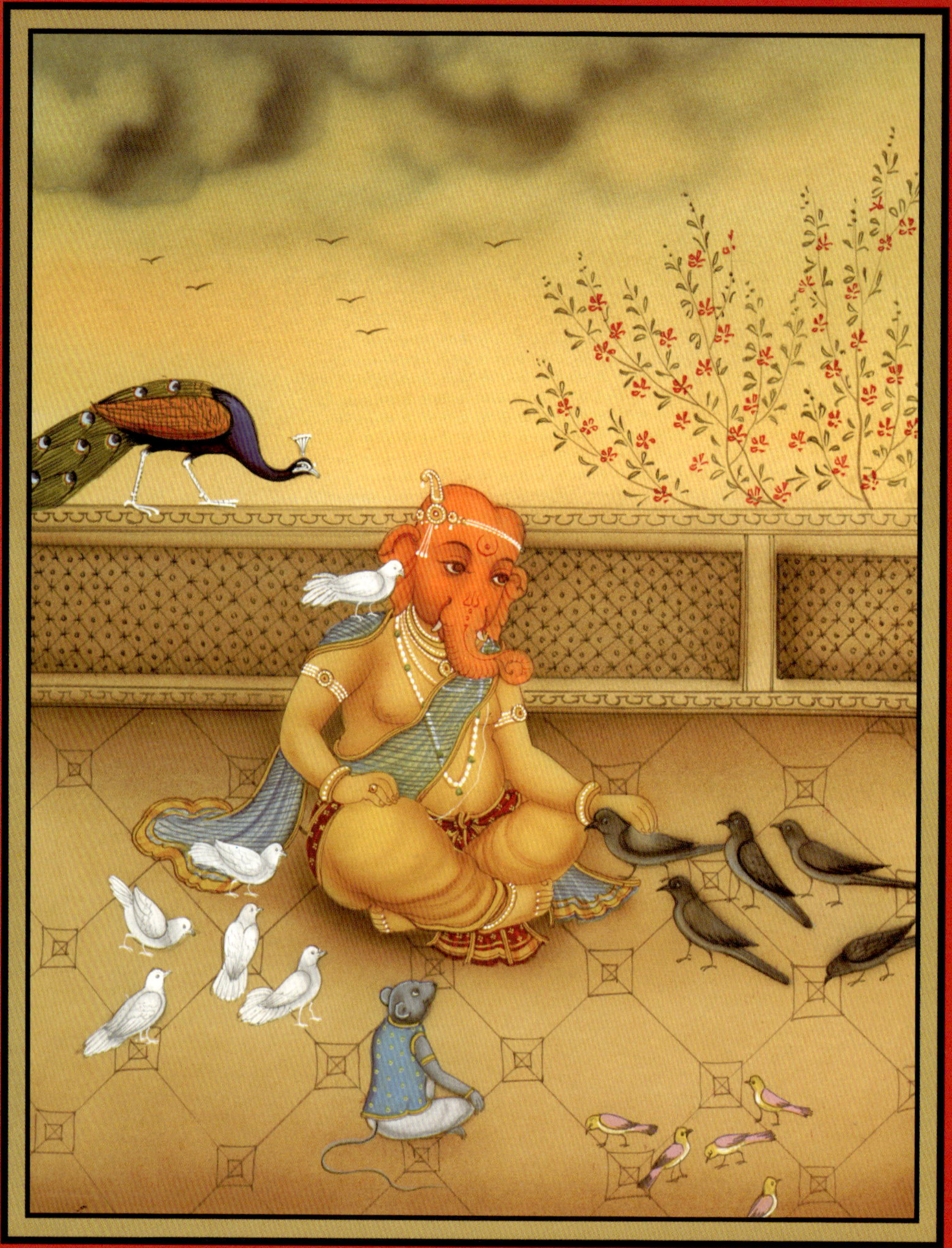

बचपन सादगी है, सुन्दरता है, भोलापन है।
बचपन में मासूमियत है, स्वच्छ निर्मल मन है।।

बचपन
Bachpan
Childhood

Childhood is simple, is beauty and is virtuous.
Childhood has innocence, purity and holy heart.

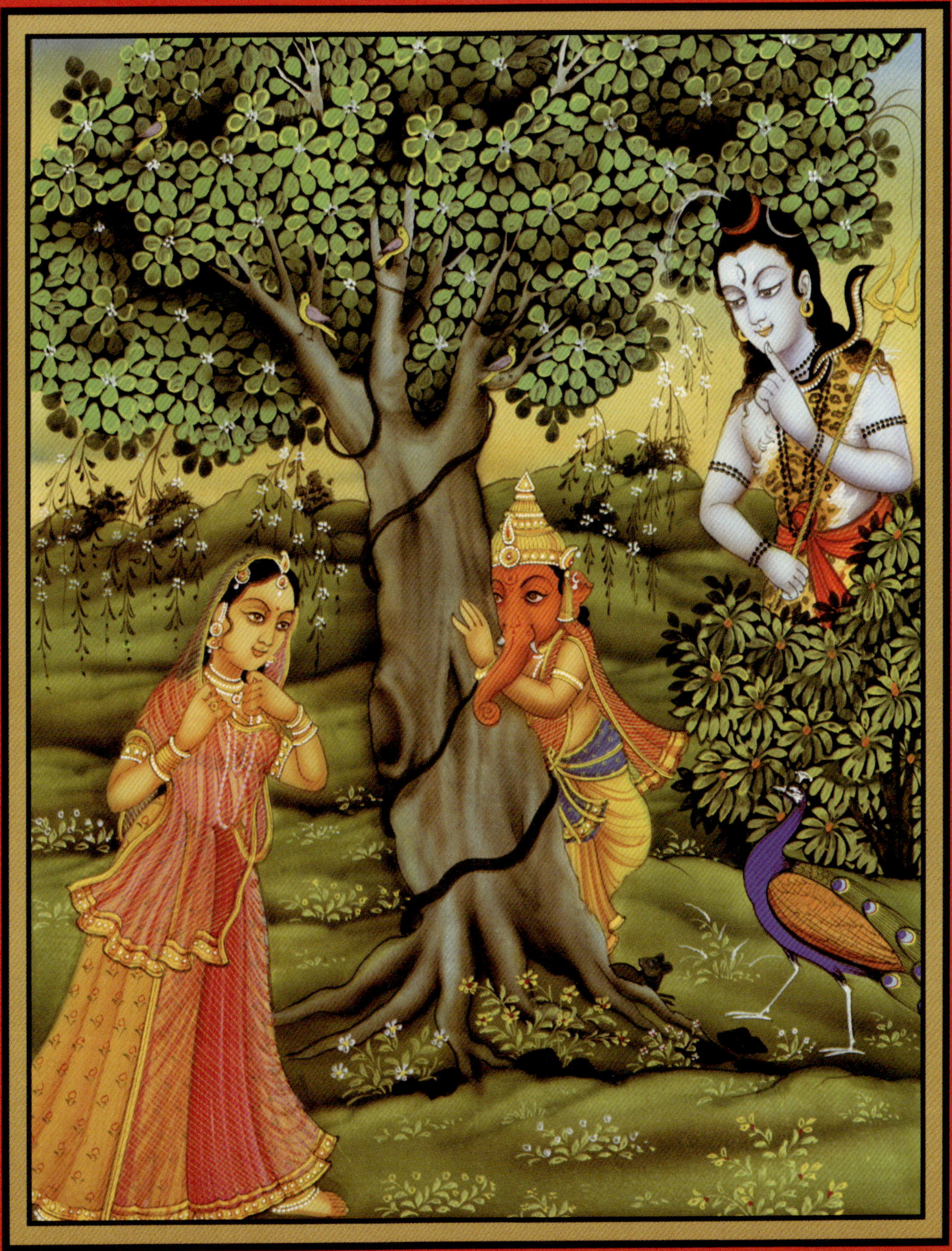

बचपन चंचल है, चपल है, मोहक है।
बचपन से ही तो हर घर में रौनक है।।

बचपन
Bachpan
Childhood

Childhood is naughty, is active and is charming.
Childhood only gives the gaiety in the family.

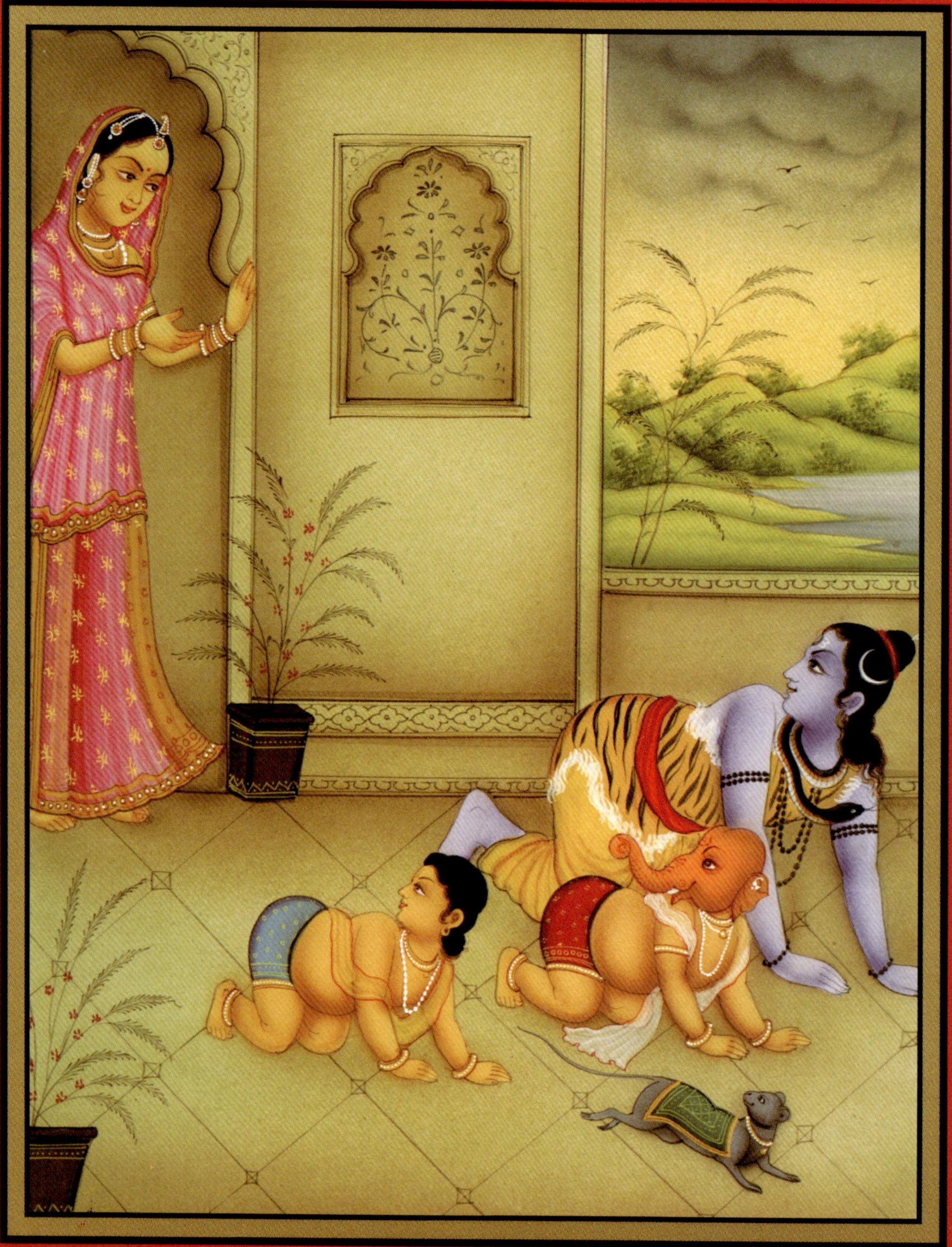

बचपन प्यारा है, न्यारा है, दुलारा है।
बचपन घर का आकर्षण, खुशियों का सहारा है।।

बचपन
Bachpan
Childhood

Childhood is fascinating, is inimitable and is lovely.
Childhood is centre of attraction and shoulder of happiness of home.

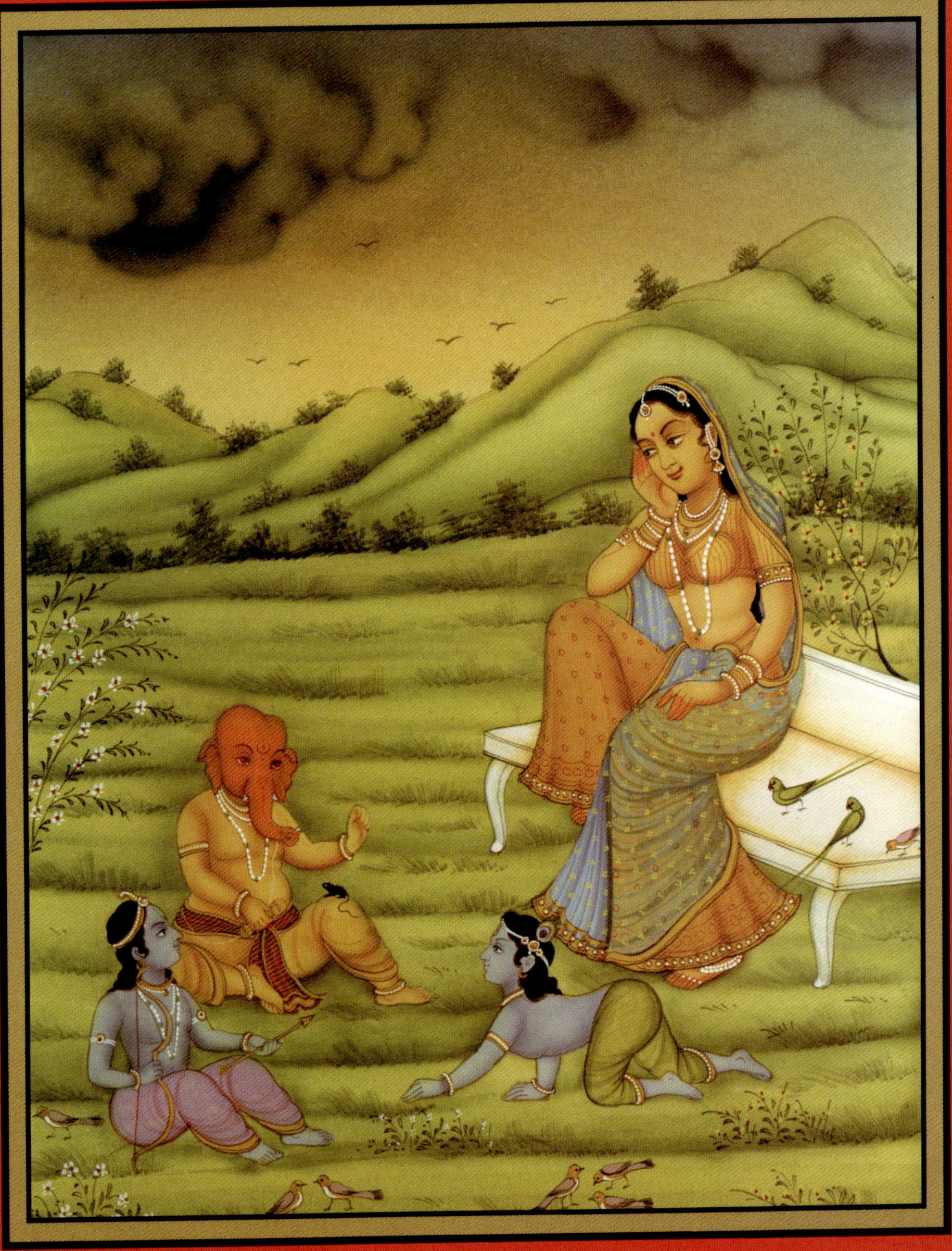

बचपन निर्मल है, निश्चल है, निर्विकार है।
बचपन परमात्मा का सबसे सुन्दर उपहार है।।

बचपन
Bachpan
Childhood

Childhood is serene, is calm and is immutable.
Childhood is the best gift of the Almighty to the world.

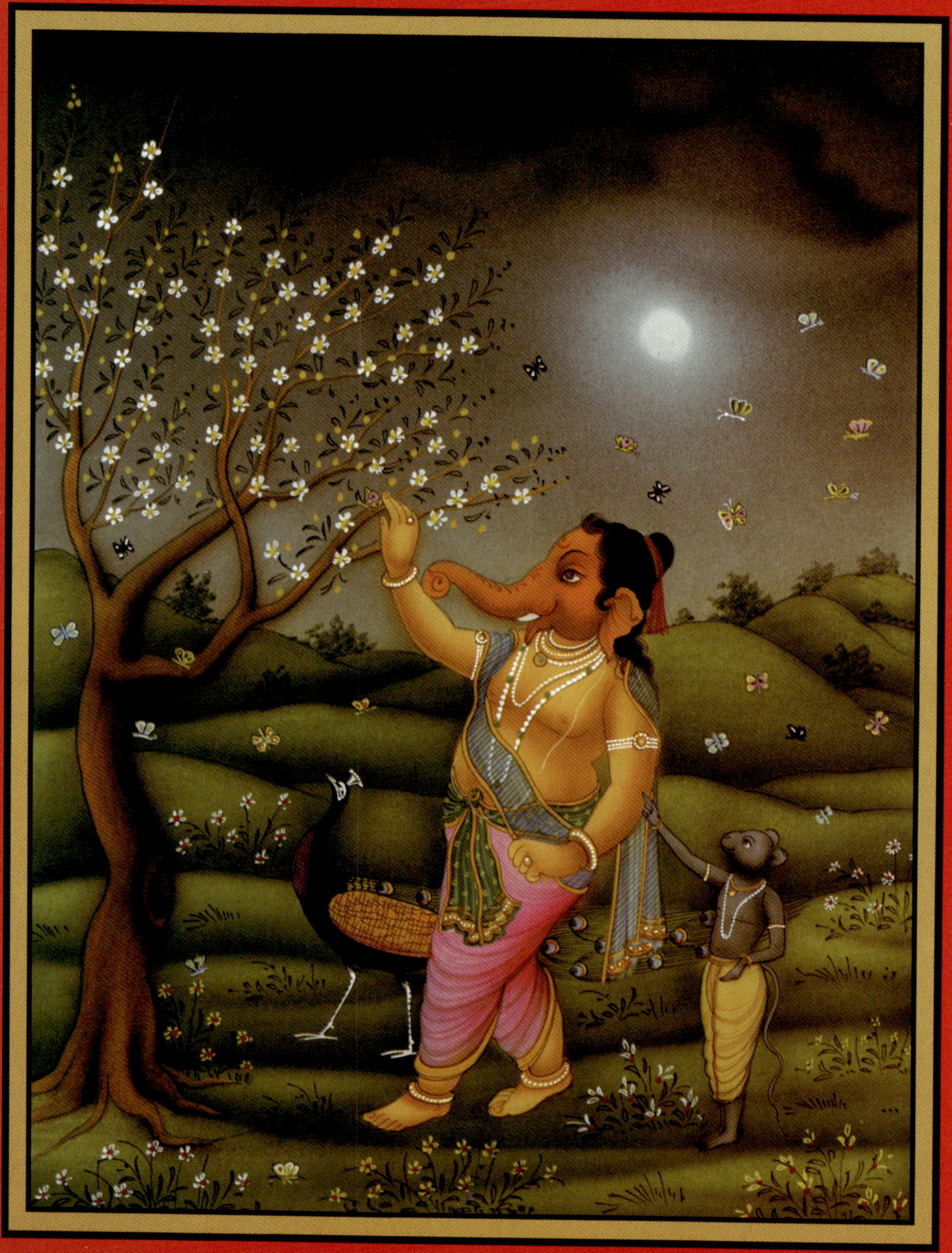

बचपन फूलों की महक और रंग-बिरंगी तितली है।
बचपन की हर अदा कुदरत के प्रेम की अभिव्यक्ति है।।

बचपन
Bachpan
Childhood

Childhood is the fragrance of the flower and multifarious butterfly.
Childhood's every action is expression of love of Supreme Being.

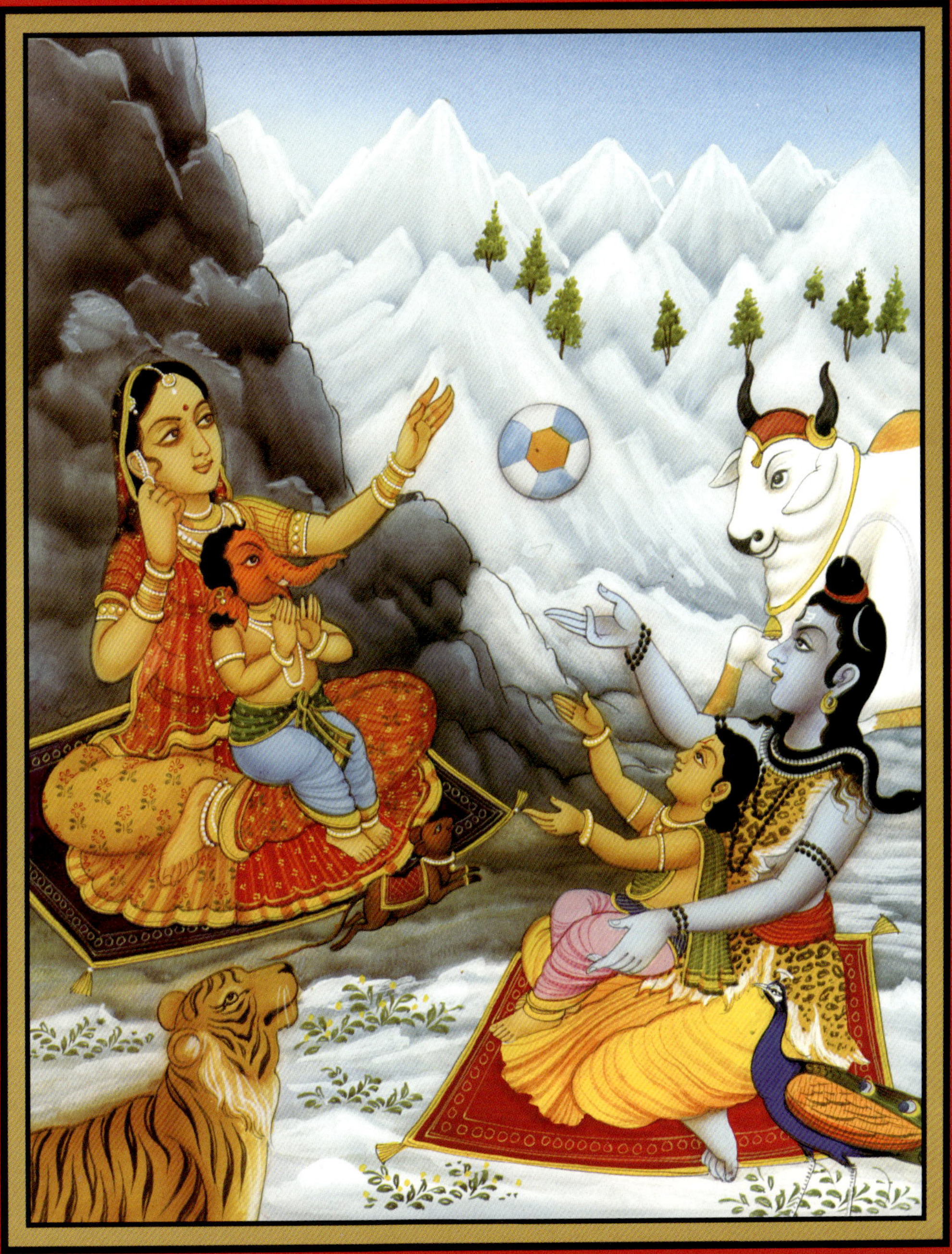

बचपन परिवार का जीवन है, विचार है, आधार है।
बचपन से छोटे और बड़े, सभी को प्यार है।।

बचपन Bachpan Childhood

Childhood is life of family, is thought and is the base.
Childhood is loved by everyone elder or younger.

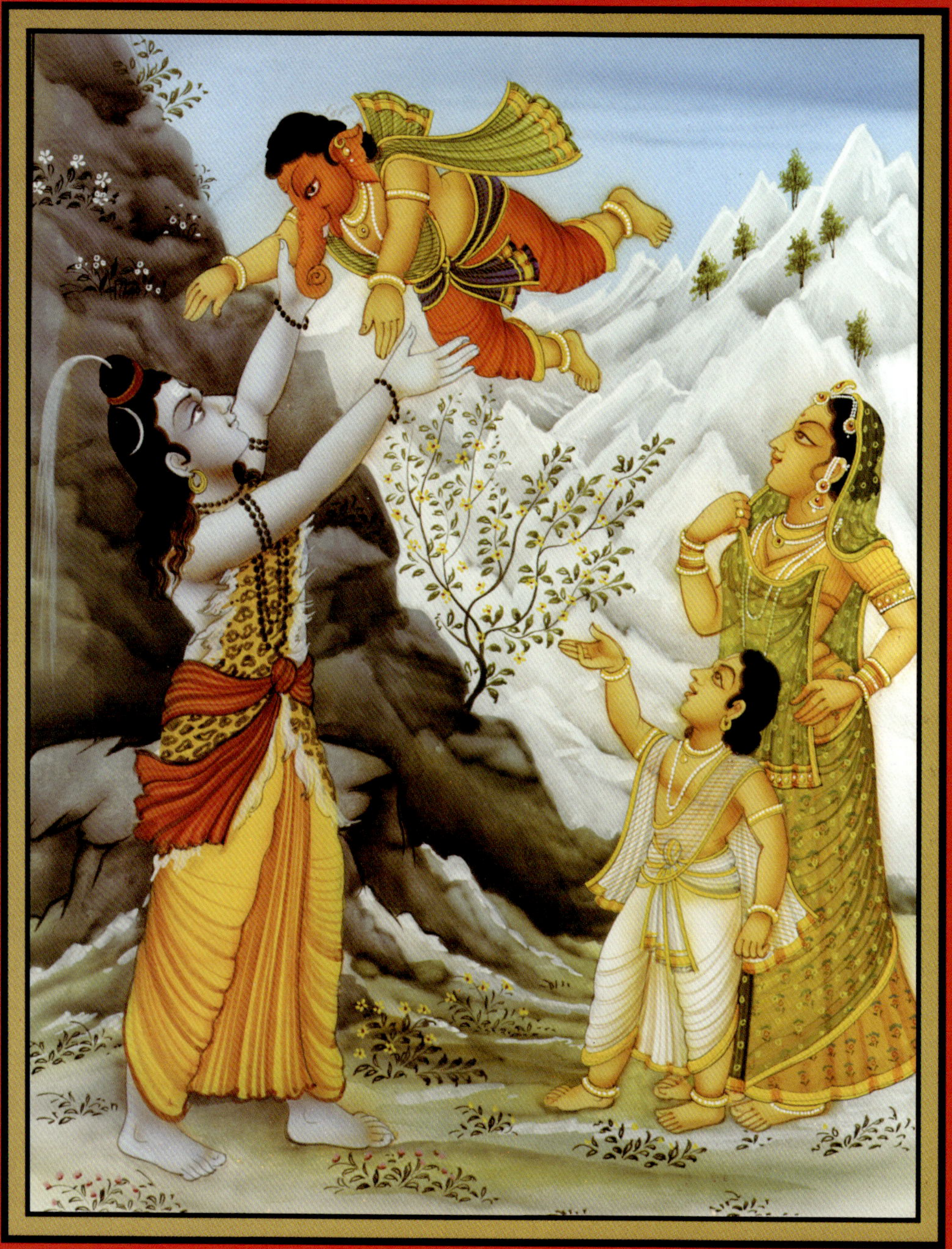

बचपन परिवार के बन्धन की डोर है।
बचपन परिवार में सभी की इच्छाओं का चोर है।।

बचपन
Bachpan
Childhood

Childhood is thread of bond in the family.
Childhood is the thief of all the desires of the family.

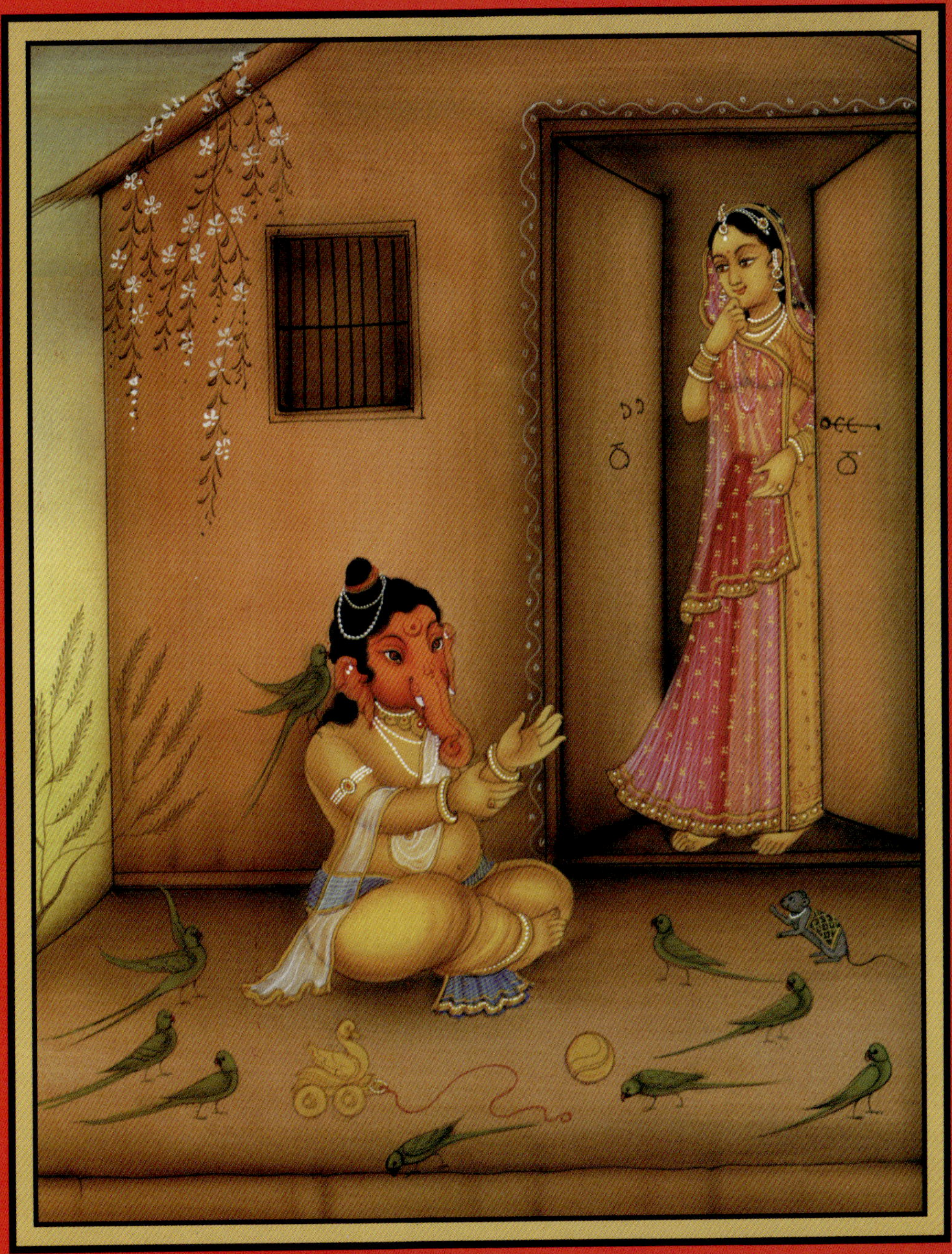

बचपन में मन शुद्ध है, साफ है, कोरा काग़ज़ है।
बचपन से परिवार में खुशियों की चमक-दमक है।।

बचपन Bachpan Childhood

Childhood's heart is clean, is clear and is plain paper.
Childhood shines the family with flash and illumination.

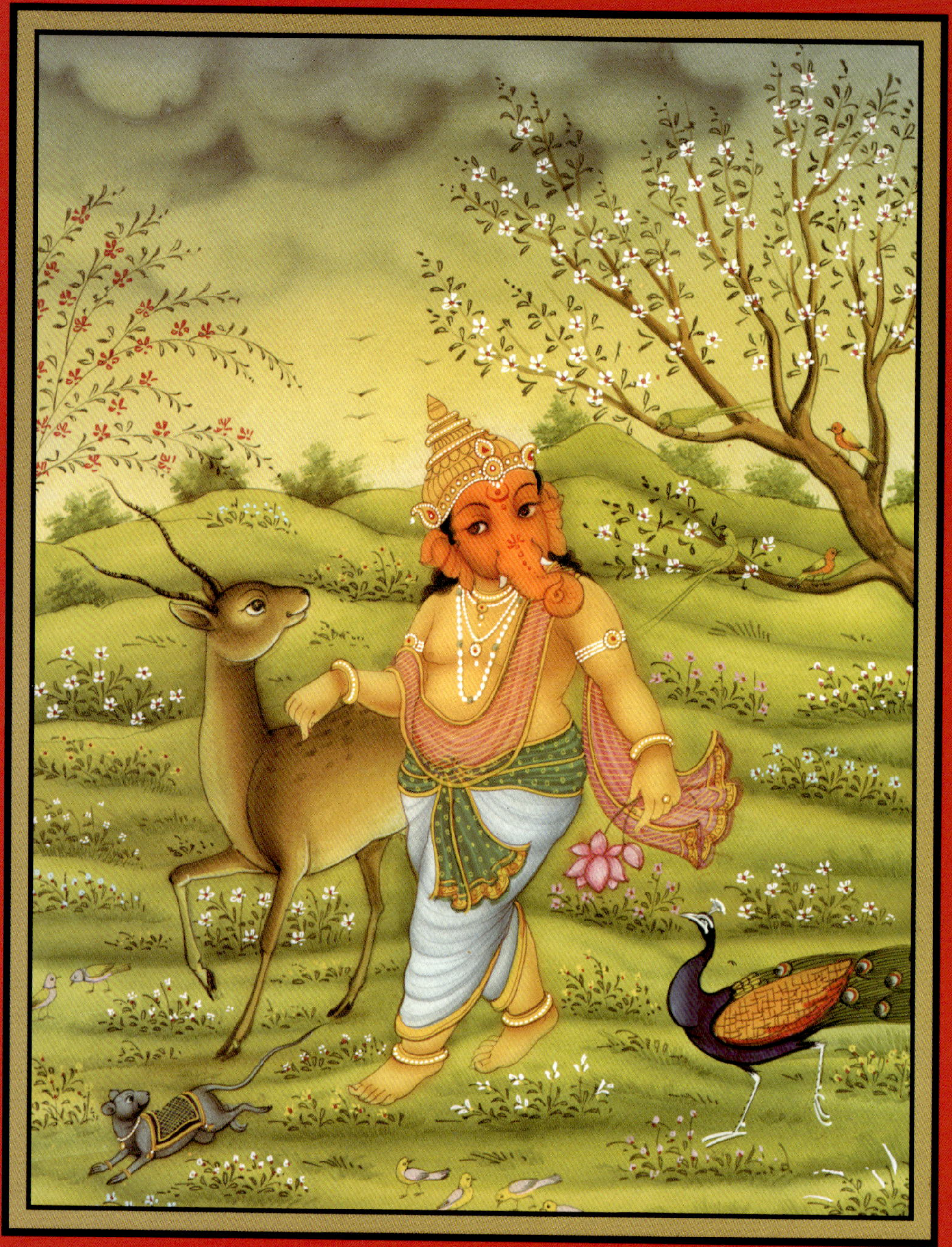

बचपन कोमलता है, महक है, मिठास है।
बचपन से ही भविष्य में जीवन की आस है।।

बचपन
Bachpan
Childhood

Childhood is effeminacy, is fragrance and is sweetness.
Childhood is expectation of the life in the future.

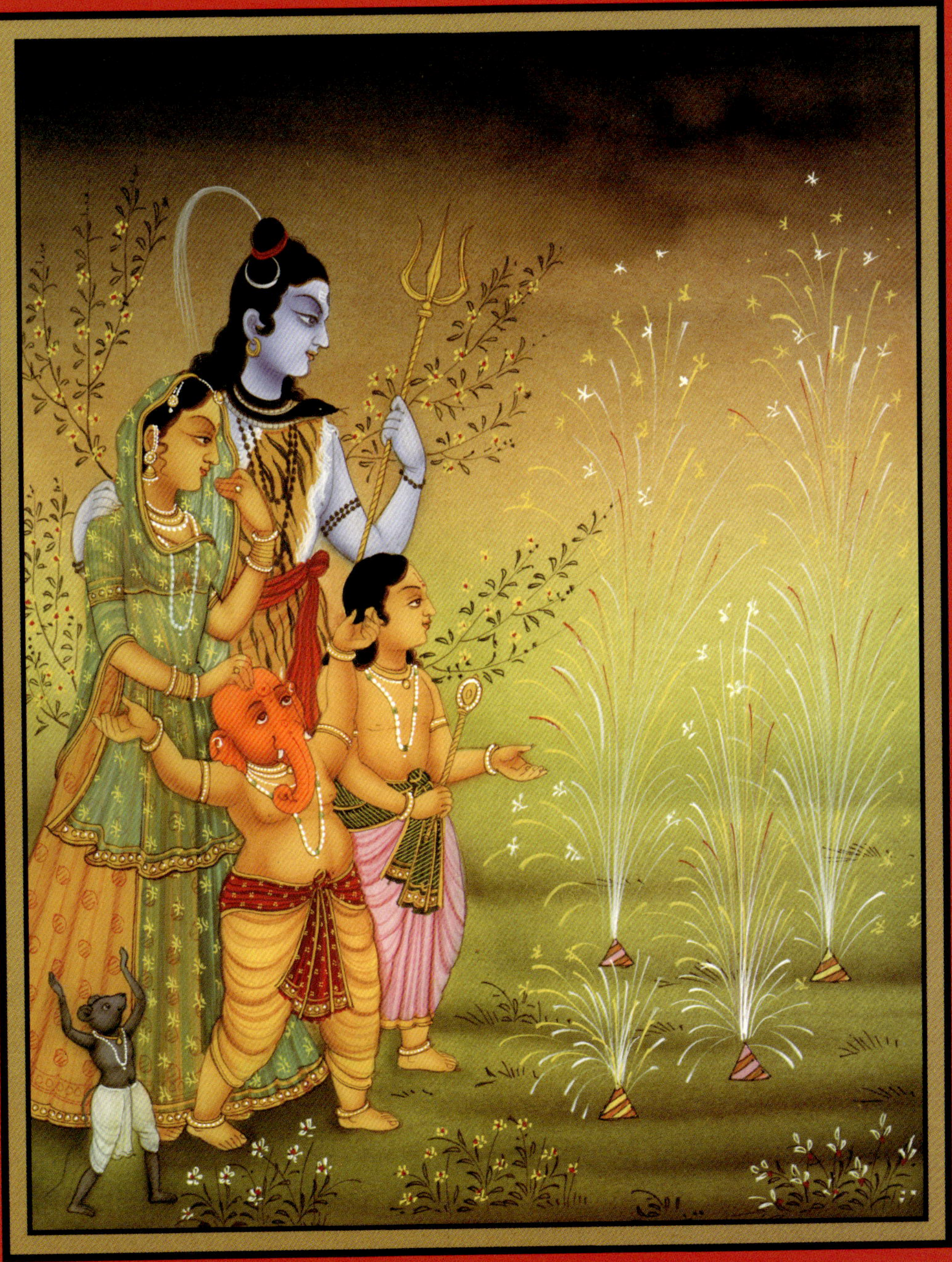

बचपन से घर में स्वर्ग है, पर्व है, त्यौहार है।
बचपन की मणियों में पिरोया सारा परिवार है।।

बचपन Bachpan Childhood

Childhood creates heaven, occasion and festival.
Childhood's jewel has interlaced the whole family.

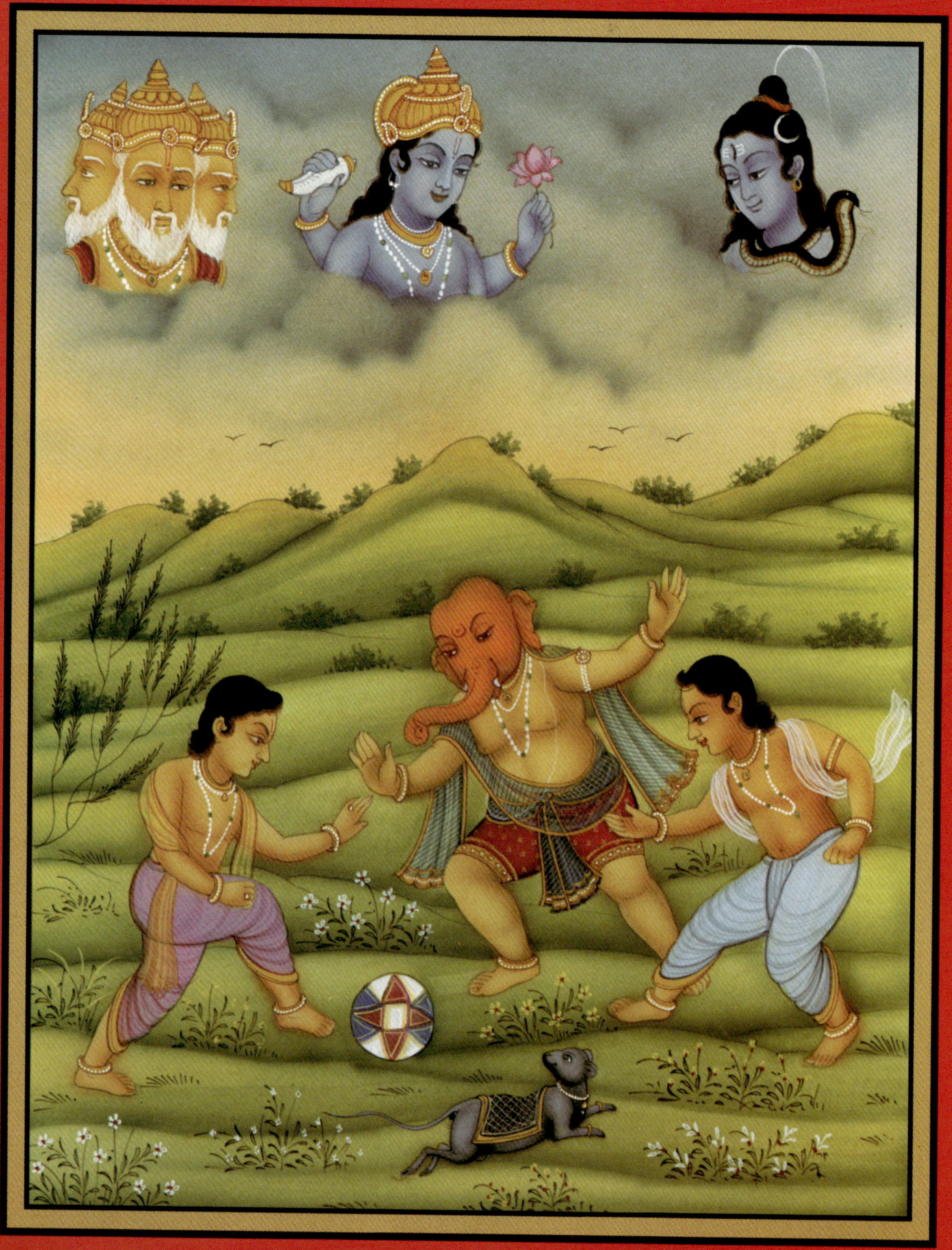

बचपन ईश्वर है, अल्लाह है, भगवान् है।
बचपन से ही चलता, प्रभु का ये जहान है।।

बचपन
Bachpan
Childhood

Childhood is Almighty, is Allah and is Omnipotent.
Childhood helps the God to run this world.

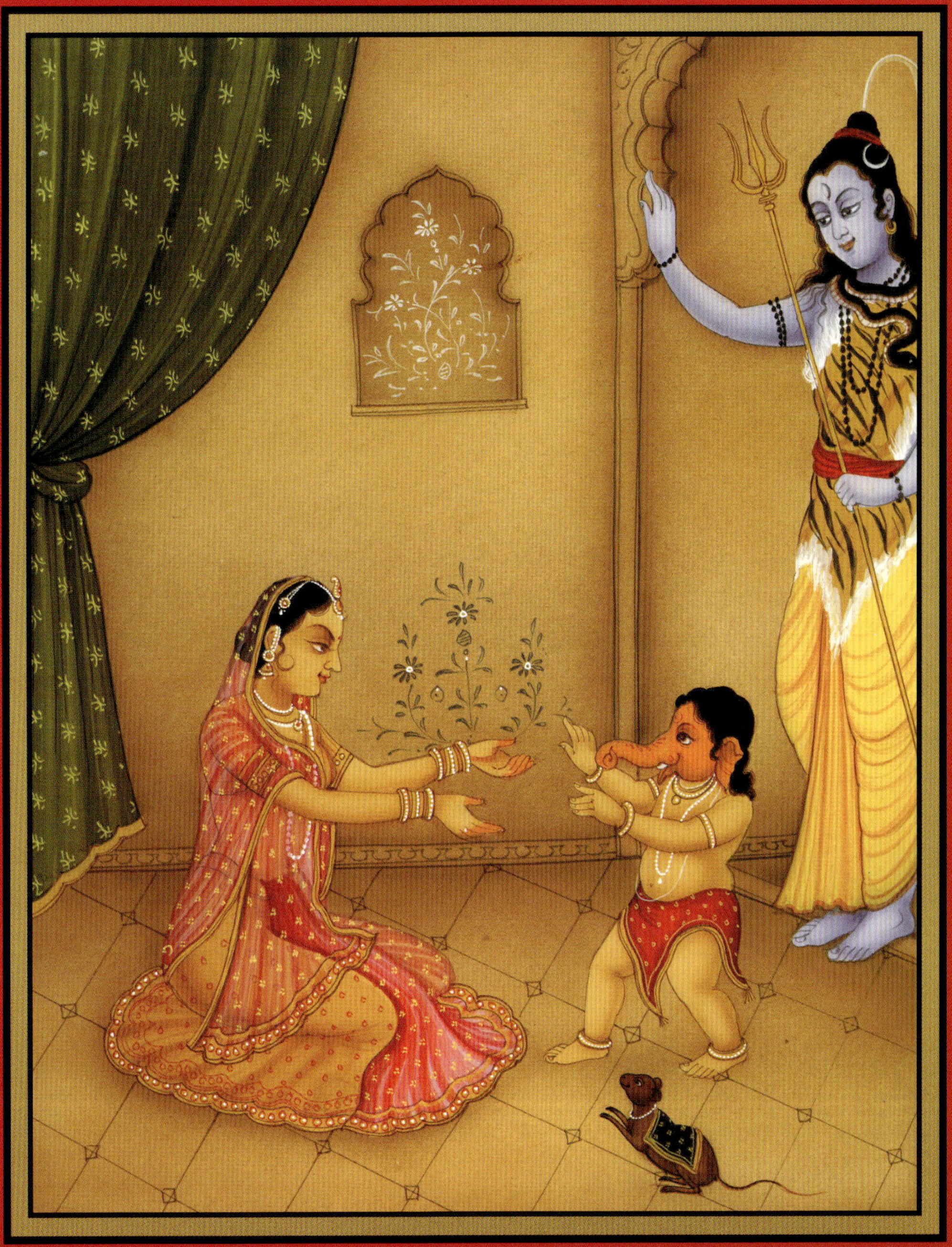

बचपन बुज़ुर्गों के प्यार का प्रतिबिम्ब है।
बचपन के रूप में ईश्वर हर घर में उपस्थित है।।

बचपन
Bachpan
Childhood

Childhood is mirror of love of elders.
Childhood makes presence of God in every home.

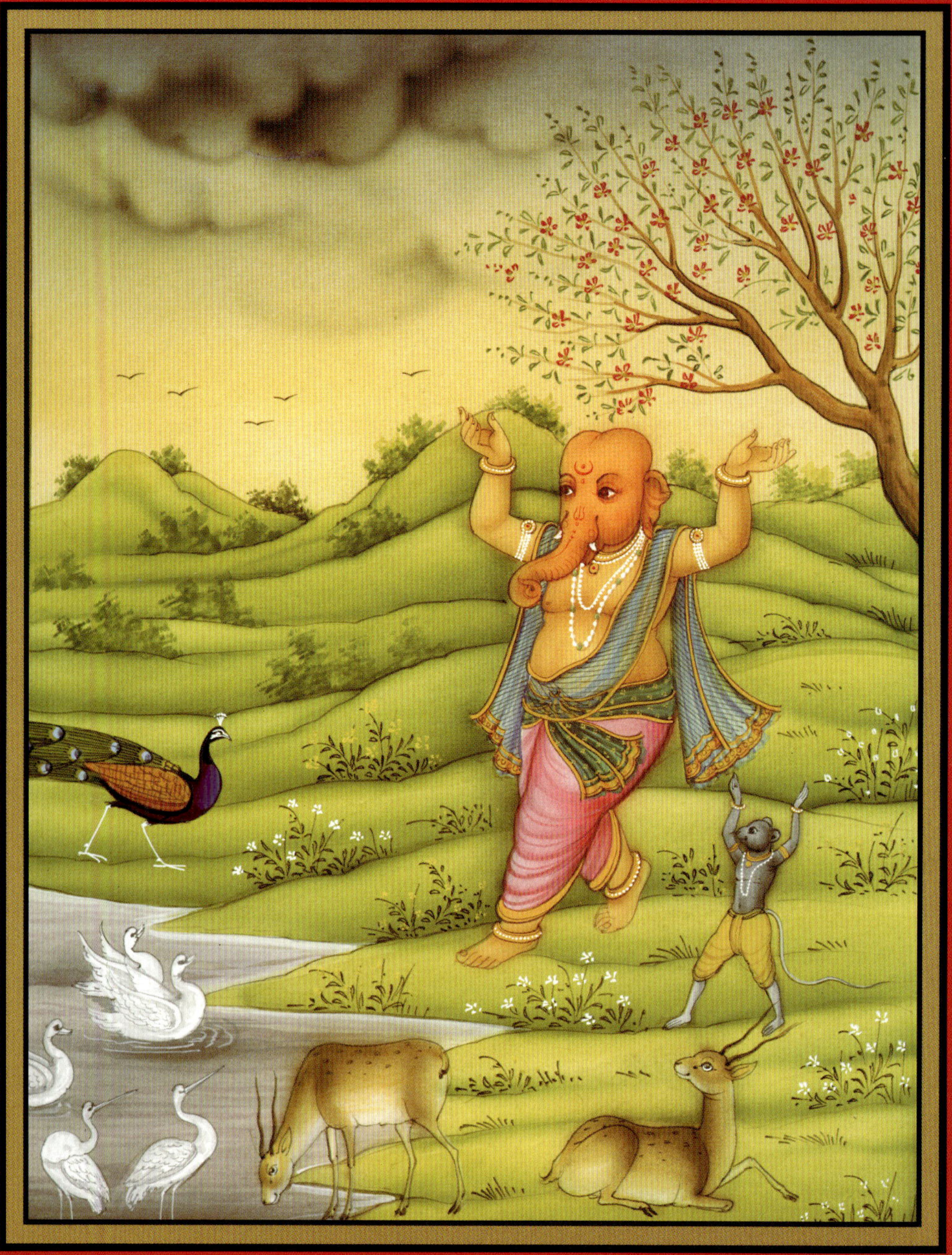

बचपन
Bachpan
Childhood

बचपन ग़मों से बेख़ौफ है, बेगाना है, अनजाना है।
बचपन मीठे संगीत पर बजने वाला प्यारा सा गाना है।।

Childhood is unaware of sorrows, is alien and is unknown.
Childhood is playing a lovely song with the sweet music.

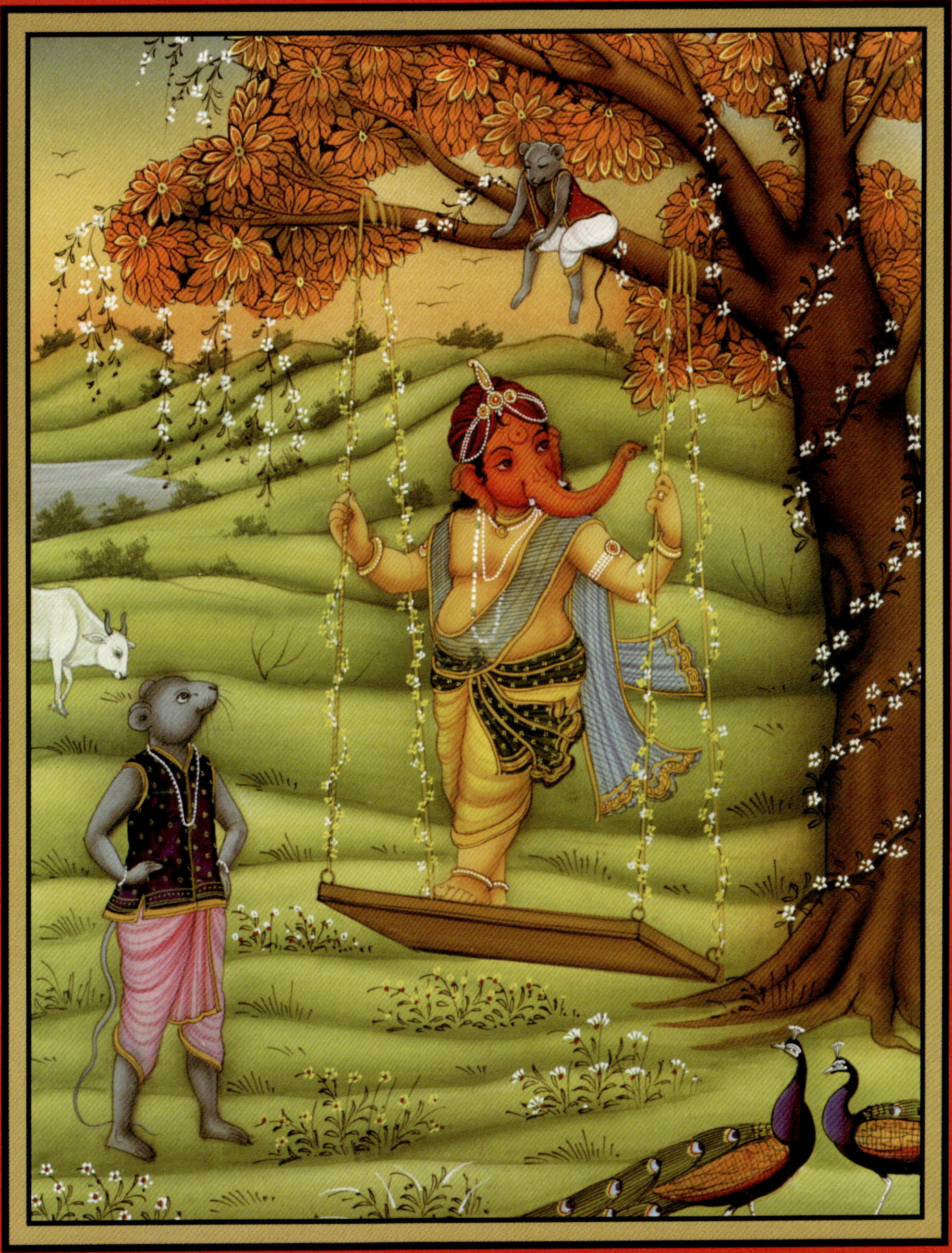

बचपन
Bachpan
Childhood

बचपन प्रभु की दया और हर बगिया का फूल है।
घर में ना हो बचपन, तो ये चुभता हुआ त्रिशूल है।।

Childhood is the mercy of God and flower of each garden.
Childhood's absence in the home is a piercing trident.

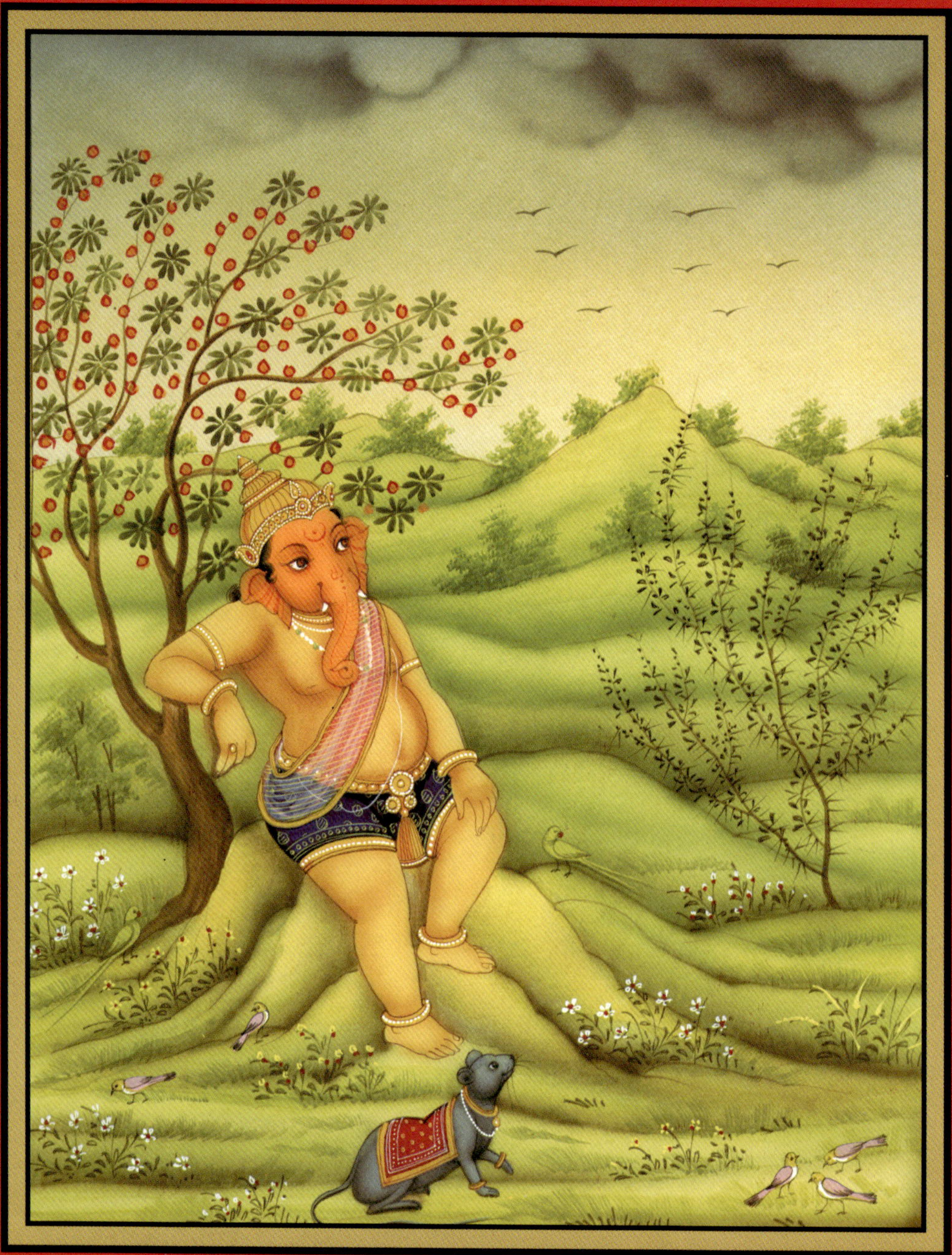

आप न सोचो कि खुशी से अकेले फूल नाचते हैं।
बचपन की तस्वीर देख साथ में बबूल नाचते हैं।।

बचपन
Bachpan
Childhood

Do not think that only flowers dance with the happiness.
Childhood makes acacia tree also dance with the flowers.

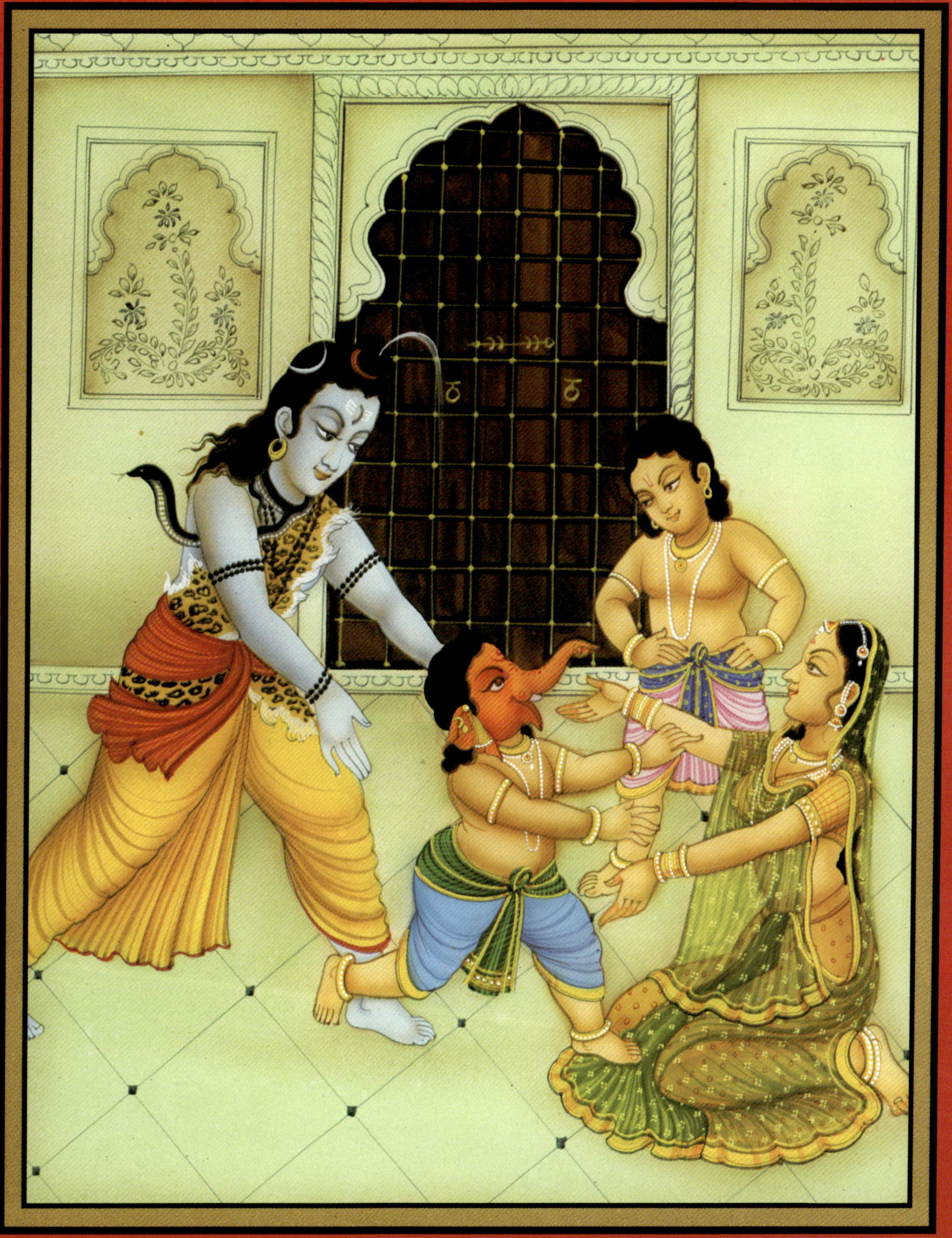

बचपन के छोटे-छोटे कदम, हर व्यक्ति का सपना है।
बचपन के मीठे बोल और तुतलाहट, वाह! क्या कहना है।।

बचपन
Bachpan
Childhood

Childhood's small steps are the dream of every person.
Childhood's sweet sound and lisping, Wah! What is to say?

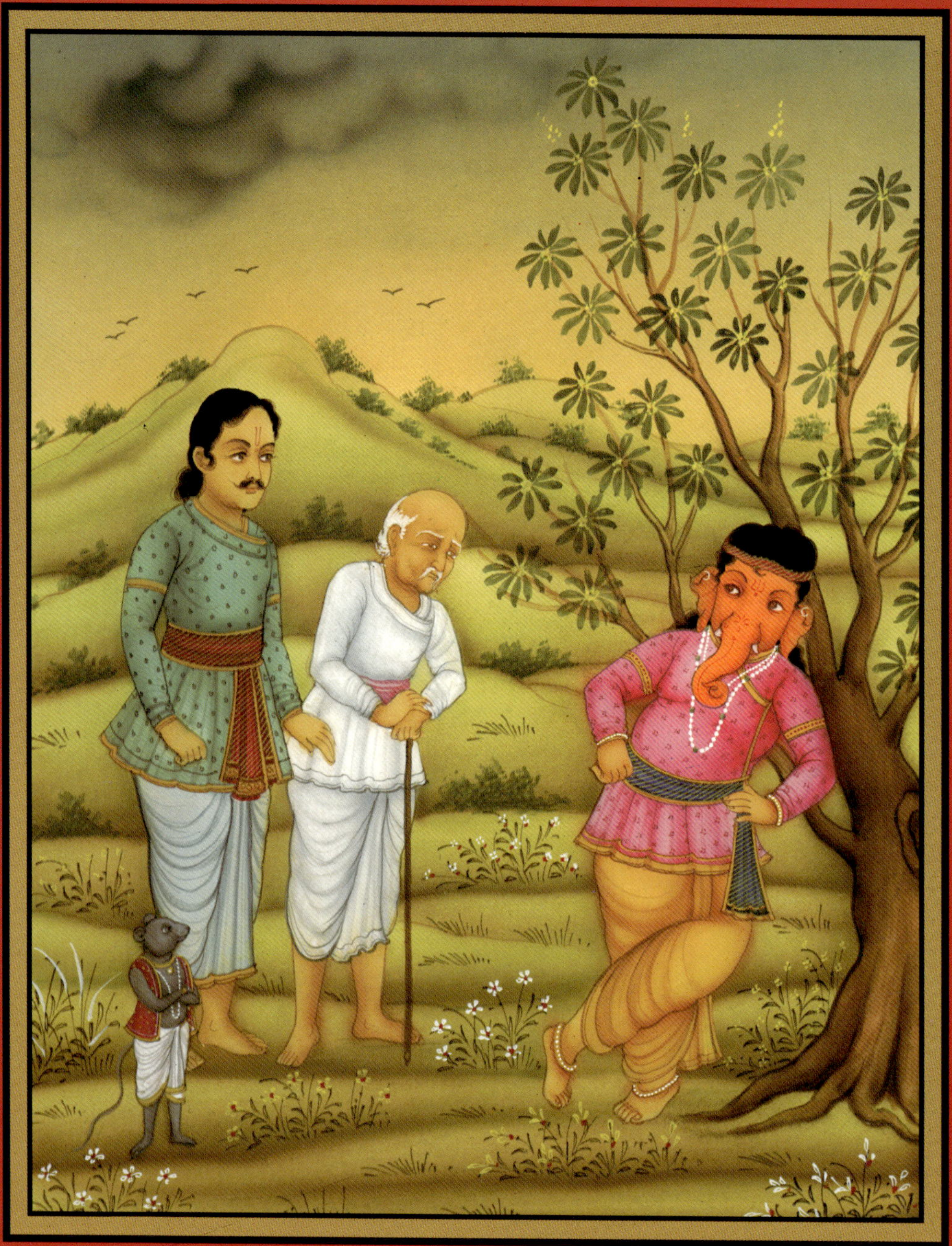

बचपन जवानी और बुढ़ापे का अतीत होता है।
ध्यान से सोचो तो सबसे अच्छा बचपन प्रतीत होता है।।

बचपन
Bachpan
Childhood

Childhood is the past of young and old age.
Childhood is the best time, if thought peacefully and carefully.

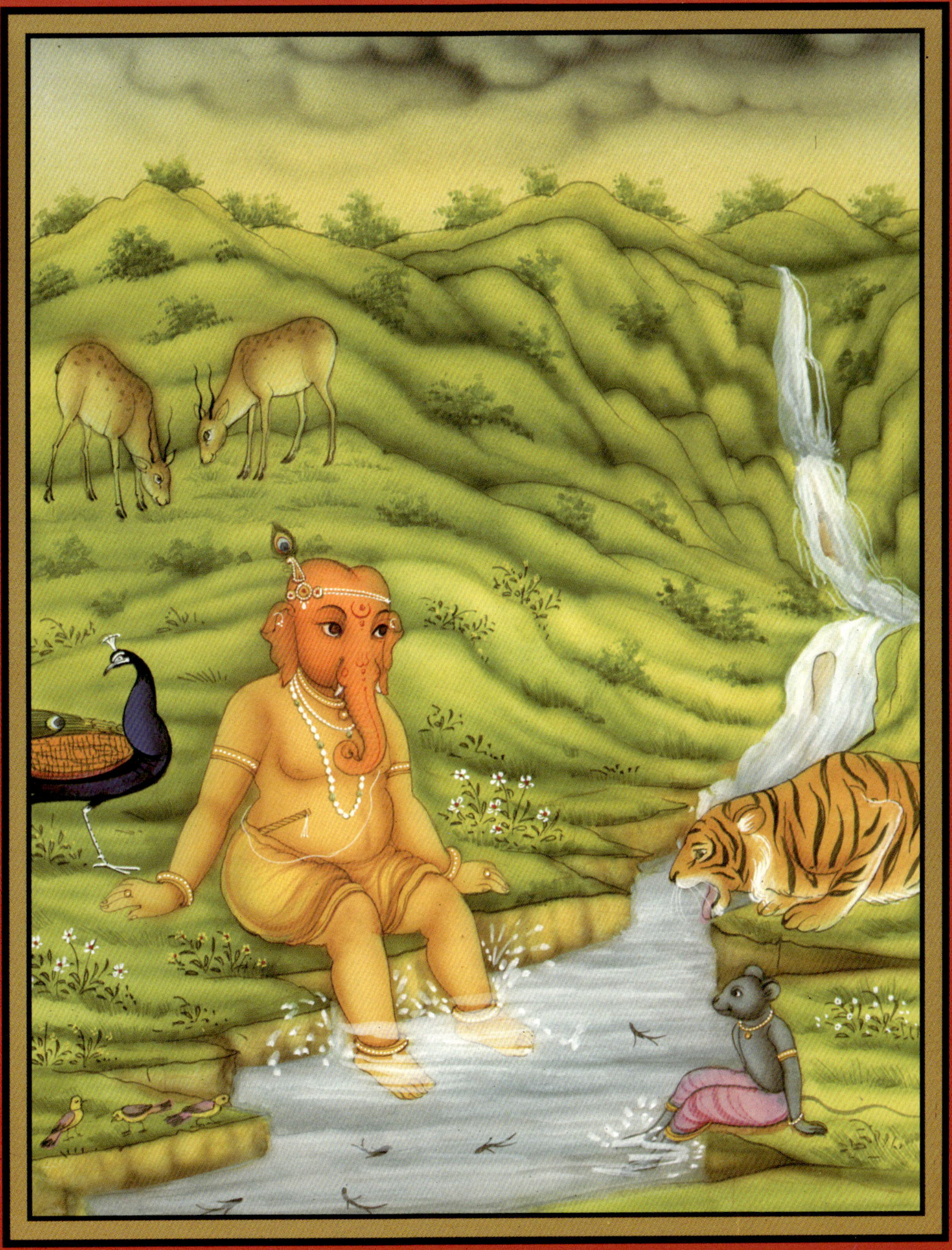

बचपन है तो ये दुनिया ज़रूर चलती रहेगी।
जैसे पानी से ये नदियां हमेशा बहती रहेंगी।।

बचपन
Bachpan
Childhood

Childhood would make the world live forever.
As water makes the rivers flow forever.

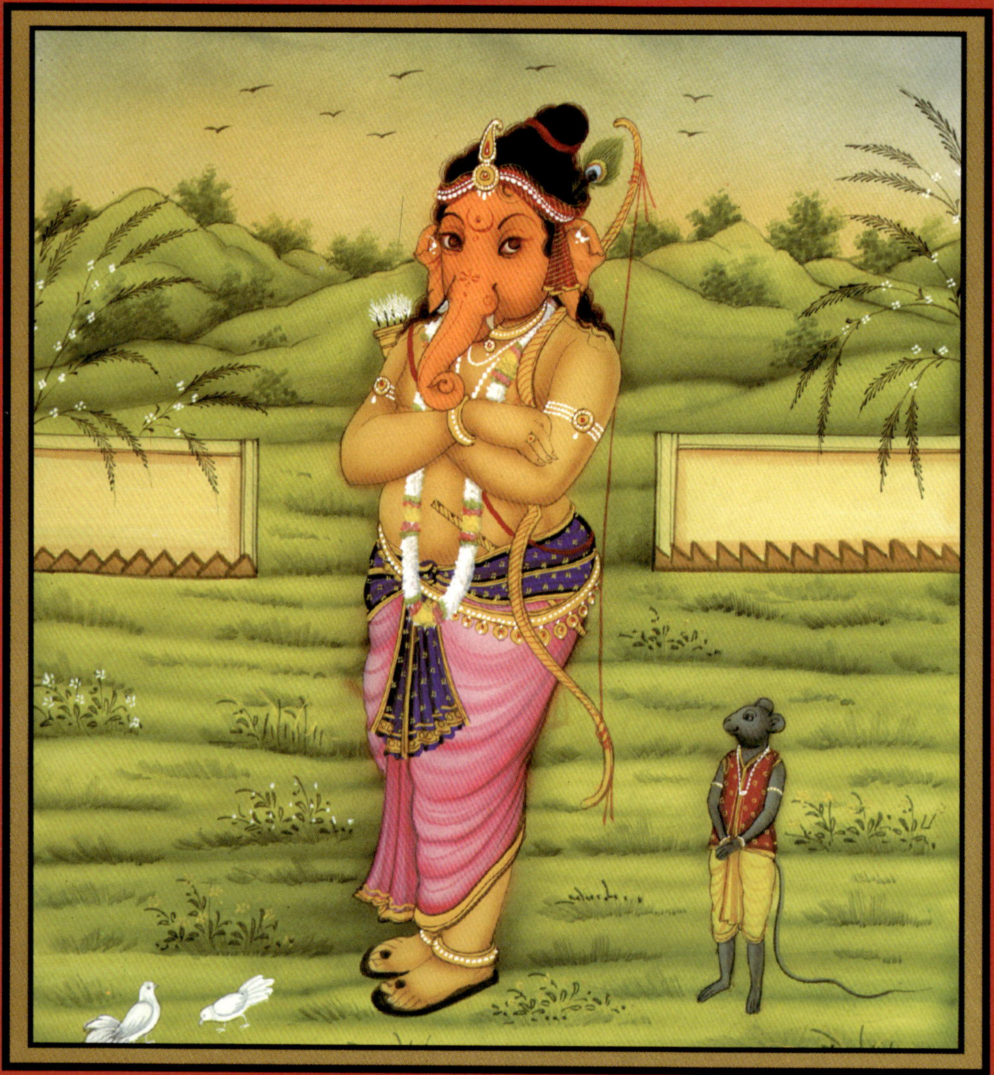

इसलिए, बचपन की सत्यता और निर्मलता को निभाओ।
बड़े होकर बड़ों के त्याग और बचपन को न भूल जाओ।।
अगर बचपन की मासूमियत और ईमान आगे भी पलता है।
तो देश में फिर रामराज्य आने से कोई रोक नहीं सकता है।।

So,
Follow the truth and serenity of the Childhood.
Don't forget the sacrifice of elders and Childhood after growing younger
If the innocence and honesty of childhood is alive
Then no one can stop arrival of power of truth (Ram Rajya) again.